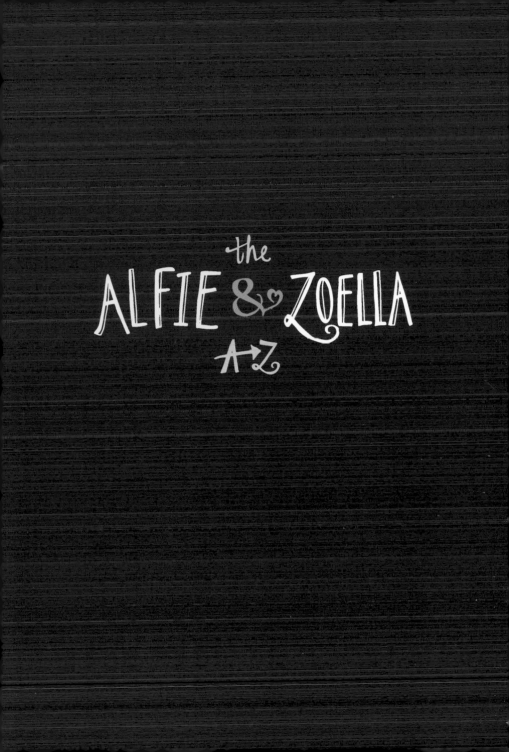

the ALFIE & ZOELLA

A→Z

The Unofficial ULTIMATE Guide to the VLOGGING SUPER-COUPLE

Jo Berry

This edition first published in Great Britain in 2015 by
Orion
an imprint of the Orion Publishing Group Ltd
Orion House, 5 Upper St Martin's Lane,
London WC2H 9EA
An Hachette UK Company

1 3 5 7 9 10 8 6 4 2

Picture credits:
David Fisher/ REX: page 12, 22 (top); Gage Skidmore: page 17; Getty: poster, page 7,
9, 14, 15, 19, 22 (bottom), 23, 24, 26, 28, 29, 37, 40, 43, 49, 52, 56, 64; Grant Falvey/ REX:
page 13 (top), 32; Matt Alexander/ PA Wire: page 16, 31, 33, 39, 50, 53 (right), 55;
Mirrorpix: page 27, 38, 53 (left), 63; Photofab/ REX: page 41; Picsol/ Corbis: page 46;
Ray Tang/ REX: page 6, 34, 62; REX: page 11, 13 (bottom), 42, 51, 58.
All other illustrations: iStock by Getty Images.

ZOELLA is the registered trade mark of Zoe Sugg.
POINTLESSBLOG is the registered trade mark of Alfie Deyes.

A CIP catalogue record for this book is available
from the British Library.

ISBN: 978 1 4091 6101 1

Designed by carrdesignstudio.com
Printed in Italy

www.orionbooks.co.uk

Contents

Meet ALFIE & ZOELLA

They are two of the most popular vloggers in the world, both with millions of subscribers each. Zoella and Alfie are both known for their fun videos that they've made together and separately, and now they're a couple in real life, too! And what a great couple they make – she's the pretty beauty and fashion blogger known for her love of car boot sales and shopping trips; he's the cheeky Brighton boy who posts fun challenges and pranks online. Together they are part of the group known as 'Generation YouTube' – a collection of popular vloggers who are the new digital stars.

As well as having fans worldwide thanks to their online posts, both Alfie and Zoella have launched themselves offline, too – Alfie wrote *The Pointless Book*, based on his YouTube videos, while Zoella has designed a range of beauty products and written *Girl Online*, the fastest-selling novel of 2014. Is there anything this amazing pair can't do? We don't think so...

ALFIE ♥

Quick Fact Download

Full name: Alfie Sydney Deyes

Nickname: His friends do sometimes call him 'Pointless'!

Date of birth: 17 September 1993

Height: 6 ft 1 in

Home town: Brighton

Favourite animal: Dog – Alfie has a black puppy pug called Nala. Growing up, he had a pet snake named Smidge.

Thing that annoys him most: People who eat really loudly, and seeing people argue.

Best friend: Alfie says he doesn't have a best friend but fellow vlogger Marcus Butler is one of Alfie's best pals, as is Jim Chapman.

Favourite food: Pasta or risotto, and Alfie's favourite chocolate bar is a Yorkie.

Favourite colour: Blue, though his favourite colour when he was little was red.

Strange talent: He can solve a Rubik's Cube in under a minute.

Star sign: Virgo

Eye colour: Brown

Hair colour: Dark brown

Phobia: Spiders! Though Alfie says it's not a phobia – he just doesn't like them.

Guilty pleasure: Clothes shopping.

Movie that made him cry: *My Sister's Keeper* with Cameron Diaz.

Most embarrassing moment: Realising his white swimming trunks had gone see-through in the water as he got out of a pool in front of his family.

Celebrity crush: Emma Watson

Fascinating fact: In 2014 Alfie bought himself a car, even though he hadn't passed his driving test or even booked an appointment to take the theory part of the test!

ZOELLA

Quick Fact Download

Full name: Zoe Elizabeth Sugg

Nickname: Zoella, Schoee (how Zoe pronounced her name when she was little).

Date of Birth: 28 March 1990

Home town: Zoe grew up in Lacock, Wiltshire, and moved to Brighton in February 2014.

Height: 5 ft 4 ½ in (that extra ½ inch is very important to Zoe)

Favourite perfume: Armani Code

Favourite animals: Guinea pigs – Zoe has two, Pippin and Percy

Best friend: Louise Pentland (Sprinkleofglitter). Louise emailed Zoe to say how much she liked her blog back in 2009 and the pair became friends. 'If blogging ended tomorrow I would be happy in the knowledge that the best thing to have come out of it was meeting Louise,' says Zoe.

Zoe is also very close to her childhood friend Alex Shipman and vlogger Tanya Burr.

Favourite food: Lemon cheesecake and rocky road ice cream... and mashed potato, which Zoe says she'll eat with anything!

Most hated food: Mushrooms

Favourite holiday spot: The Maldives and the Greek islands.

Phobias: Vomit, spiders... and the sea! ('I don't trust what's in it.')

Strange talent: Zoe used to do maypole and country dancing in primary school.

Star sign: Aries

Eye colour: Blue

Hair colour: Brown

Favourite actors: Will Smith, Orlando Bloom, Ashton Kutcher

Favourite movies: *The Notebook* and *Moulin Rouge*

Favourite books: *The Diary of Anne Frank* and *Lots of Love* by Fiona Walker

Fascinating fact: Zoe was in the first two Harry Potter movies because the filmmakers used her primary school in the movie. She was 10 years old and was an extra, pretending to be in Hufflepuff house. Sadly you can't spot her in either movie!

Celebrity crush: Evan Peters

The Early Days

We know lots about Alfie and Zoe from their vlogs, but here's a little insight into their lives before they discovered YouTube...

ALFIE

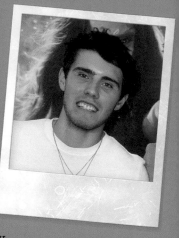

On the 17 September 1993 in London, little Alfie Deyes popped into the world. When he was four, Alfie, his sister and parents moved to Brighton, on the south coast of England. It was there that he went to primary school, where Alfie's main memory is of crying in every school stage performance he was in!

As we know from his YouTube videos, Alfie is quite athletic, and from the age of 11 until he was 15 he did competitive gymnastics, and even won a competition featuring kids from the entire county. He was popular at school and loved it, and it was while in secondary school in 2009 that he recorded his first YouTube video – without telling any of his friends. It wasn't until months later, when Alfie had a few thousand followers and someone recognised him on the street, that his friends finally found out!

Alfie went to college after secondary school, but wasn't happy with the subjects he chose to study. Never one to quit, he continued to work hard and get the grades he needed to go to university and he won a place at the one he wanted to go to. First, though, it was time to have some fun and in 2012 Alfie decided to have a gap year so he could travel and spend more time working on his vlog.

ZOE

Born on 28 March 1990 and weighing just over six pounds, Zoe made an impression from the moment she was born: 'the second my head popped out, I opened my eyes and blinked at my dad, and it really scared him!' Eighteen months later, Zoe's brother Joseph was born and the family grew up in a small village in Wiltshire together. Zoe's best friend at primary school was Alex, and it was Alex holding the camera when Zoe first started making videos of herself 'doing random silliness' when she was 10 years old.

It was when she was 10 that Zoe got her first taste of celebrity life, too. She was cast in *Harry Potter and the Philosopher's Stone*, and got to spend time with a lot of the cast including Daniel Radcliffe, Emma Watson and Rupert Grint. Zoe was actually in the first two movies – but her scenes as an extra at Hogwarts never made it into the final movie. Shame!

Then it was off to secondary school, where Zoe got A-grades in her Art, Textiles and Photography A-levels but wasn't sure what she wanted to do when she left school. While some of her friends went off to university, or stayed local but met up a lot to go out, Zoe suffered from anxiety attacks so felt she couldn't join in. It made work difficult, too, and while she had a job in retail and then one in interior design, she wasn't happy. To cheer herself up, in 2009 Zoe started going online and writing a blog, and occasionally making YouTube videos. And so Zoella was born.

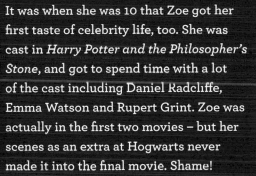

THE *Vlogging* *life*

Both Alfie and Zoe began posting videos on YouTube in 2009, but their journeys to *vlogger mega-stardom* have been quite different. Zoe began by watching other people's make-up tutorials and reading BEAUTY BLOGS, until she felt confident enough to start writing her own blog and later post videos online. It wasn't long after Zoe started posting online that she was contacted by Louise Pentland (sprinkleofglitter), who told Zoe how much she liked her blog. The pair became friends and have emailed or chatted every day since.

Soon, Zoe's video posts became more and more popular. By the end of 2009, Zoe had a thousand followers, and in 2013 that number had gone up to ONE MILLION! But while her online life was great, and she made friends among the vlogging community with people like Alfie, Tanya Burr and Tyler Oakley, her life off camera wasn't so happy. In 2012, Zoe ended a relationship with her long-term boyfriend, and her parents also divorced. The two events meant she had more panic attacks than normal, but also spurred her on to spend

more time posting on YouTube and led to her making loads of great friends online. It also meant her first trip on a plane for seven years when she went to *Florida* to meet lots of fellow vloggers at Playlist Live, the YouTube convention.

Alfie, meanwhile, was travelling a lot as well, thanks to his successful Pointlessblog, which had grown from short little videos of a teenage Alfie talking about whatever came into his head, into a collection of challenges and chats such as *120 Chicken Nuggets in 20 Minutes*, the WHIPPED CREAM CHALLENGE and collaborations with fellow YouTube friends. During his gap year, he went to *Los Angeles* for Vidcon 2012, then New York, and then to Florida for Playlist 2013, and he moved house too, leaving his family in Brighton to move in with pal Caspar Lee in London in 2013.

Of course, the biggest change in friends Alfie and Zoe's lives was just around the corner...

AWARDS AND MILESTONES

October 2011 Zoe wins the 2011 Cosmopolitan Blog Award for Best Established Beauty Blog

October 2012 Zoe wins the 2012 Cosmopolitan Best Beauty Vlogger Award

August 2013 Zoella reaches 2 million subscribers

October 2013 Zoe wins the Best British Vlogger Award at the Radio 1 Teen Awards

October 2013 Alfie and Zoe are both named as two of the most influential Tweeters in the UK

December 2013 Alfie posts his video of singer Ariana Grande doing his make-up on YouTube and it is nominated for a Teen Choice Award. It's had more than 7 million views, too

January 2014 Alfie, along with Jim Chapman, Marcus Butler and Caspar Lee, get their own YouTube chat show, The Crew

April 2014 Zoe wins the UK Favourite Vlogger at the Nickolodeon Kids Choice Awards

September 2014 Zoe launches her Zoella Beauty products.

September 2014 Pointlessblog reaches 3 million subscribers

September 2014 Alfie's *The Pointless Book* is published

October 2014 Alfie appears on The Radio 1 Breakfast Show with vlogger Marcus Butler

October 2014 Zoe wins the Best British Vlogger Award at the Radio 1 Teen Awards again!

November 2014 Zoe's first novel, *Girl Online*, is published and has the highest ever first-week sale for a debut author since records began in 1998

November 2014 Alfie and Zoe are invited to join stars like One Direction and U2 and sing on the charity single 'Do They Know It's Christmas?', for the Band Aid 30 campaign

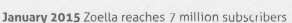

January 2015 Zoella reaches 7 million subscribers

ALFIE Antics

Alfie, always the prankster, loves to accept challenges dreamt up by his friends and the fans of Pointlessblog. The best ones are the ones where he is doing silly stuff, like getting a plate of whipped cream smeared on his face when he gets a question about Zoe wrong, or trying out yoga wearing women's yoga clothes.

Remember, if you are thinking of a challenge or prank to do, pick one that will make your friends laugh, not one that will make them cross or upset! It's often much funnier if you're the subject of the joke – don't make fun of your friends as they may not like it (how would you feel if someone super-glued your expensive phone to the ceiling?) and only include them in a prank if they really want to do it!

THE 7-SECOND CHALLENGE!

Take it in turns to challenge your friends to do something... anything... but they only have 7 seconds to do it in! (You'll need a clock timer or phone timer for this one.)

This can be done with just a couple of people or a whole group – one person challenges the others to do, for example, a handstand in 7 seconds, and then the others have to try!

You score this one by winning a point for every challenge completed, with the person with the most points at the end becoming the winner.

Want some more suggestions of challenges you can do in 7 seconds? How about say the alphabet, do a cartwheel, throw a ball through a hoop five times, butter a piece of bread, eat 10 marshmallows, do a friend's eye make-up, draw a friend's portrait...

The 1-Minute
SPOT THE DIFFERENCE
CHALLENGE

You have 1 minute to spot
the 5 differences
between the photos.

Go!

Answers on page 64.

Falling in love

While they share an awful lot of their lives online, Alfie and Zoe managed to keep one thing secret from their fans, at least for a little while – the fact that in 2013 the two friends had started dating.

In fact, no one would have found out for a while if it hadn't been for eagle-eyed YouTube viewers who spotted Zoe's laptop background in a vlog by her friend Jim Chapman – and that background was a photo taken on holiday of Zoe and Alfie together. Fans of both of them had imagined that 'Zalfie' existed for quite a while – even when the two were just friends – so when the photo was spotted, Zoe and Alfie's public Facebook and Twitter accounts went into meltdown as fans discussed whether this was a sign that the two of them were an item.

The speculation came as a surprise to them both, as neither Zoe or Alfie had thought about revealing their relationship to their fans, nor what they would do if their secret came out. In the end, Zoe published a post on her Zoella blog in August 2013, confirming that she and Alfie were dating and explaining just why they had kept it private.

'We decided to keep it to ourselves and hang back a bit until we were ready to chat about it with you all,' she wrote. Most fans supported their decision, especially as Zoe explained that all the attention was affecting their friends, too – 'Zalfie' fans were commenting on any and every video

ALF ♡ ZO

either Zoe or Alfie appeared in, speculating on how they looked at each other, and not commenting on the actual videos themselves! Of course, some fans were cross that they had been kept in the dark, but Zoe went on to add that she and Alfie didn't want to become an 'online couple'.

> We decided to KEEP IT TO OURSELVES and hang back a bit until we were ready to chat about it with you all.

Once the initial attention died down, Zoe and Alfie got on with their romance... privately! In February 2014, with Alfie back living in Brighton, Zoe moved to her own flat to be nearer him, and eight months later the pair revealed a secret that everyone had been waiting for – Zalfie was now living together!

Of course, they now feature in each other's videos more than they did when they were just friends, and we've watched Alfie be the best boyfriend ever (his words!) when he bought her a Nando's takeaway, or Zoe and him chatting in bed. In July 2014 they even addressed a fan's speculation that Alfie was planning to propose, with Zoe showing her bare hands to prove there was no engagement ring! If it ever is to happen (after all, they're both young), we're sure their followers will be the first to know!

THE FRIEND ZONE

Both Alfie and Zoe have talked about who inspires them, and they agree that the people who mean the most to them are their friends, including their vlogging pals. Here's a guide to just some of their bestest, closest and most influential friends... and you'll recognise most of them because they often appear in the Zoella and Pointlessblog vlogs!

Joe Zoe's younger brother Joe Sugg is known as ThatcherJoe online — probably because he worked as a roof thatcher as well as posting YouTube videos in his spare time! He created his channel back in November 2011 and has over three million subscribers who watch his challenges and pranks. Joe lives in London with pal Caspar Lee, who must be a very patient roommate since Joe's pranks have included covering a room in tin foil, and on another occasion, completely filling it with balloons.

Caspar Caspar Lee was in South Africa, and since coming to England, where he was born, he has lived with both Alfie and now Joe. He started his YouTube channel 'Caspar' in 2010 and is best known for pranks and comedy sketches, and interviews with fellow YouTubers. He's even tried acting, appearing in a movie called *Spud 3* with British comic acting legend John Cleese.

Jim Jim Chapman is best known for his advice Q&As and videos, including the popular 'A Guys' Advice For Girls' series. He's got a degree in psychology, so often gives good advice when he isn't joining in with videos with his friends. Jim is engaged to Tanya Burr, and it was during one of his vlogs that Zalfie fans spotted a photo in the background (on Zoe's laptop) of Zoe and Alfie together that led to everyone guessing they were a couple.

Louise

Zoe first connected with Louise, Pentland (better known as sprinkleofglitter) online in 2009, and the two became close friends (they call themselves Chummy). Louise started her online career writing a craft and interior blog, and then focused on beauty and shopping — and her pregnancy — when she began her YouTube channel in 2010. Her daughter Darcy (who she used to call Baby Glitter in her videos) was born in April 2011 and sometimes features in Louise's videos.

Anna and Jonathan

Known as the 'Sacconejolys' — a combination of their surnames — American Anna Saconne and Dubliner Jonathan Joly live in Ireland and upload videos about their life (including two young children) every day. They are friends with both Zoe and Alfie — and even videoed Zalfie looking after their children, Eduardo and Emilia.

Marcus

Alfie's pal Marcus Butler also lives in Brighton. He began his YouTube journey creating music mixes and posting them online and is now well known for his challenge videos, including the 'eggs to the face' quiz that he did with Alfie. He's got his own clothing line and lives with YouTube style vlogger Niomi Smart.

Tanya

Tanya Burr, like Zoe, is well known for her beauty advice online. She started off working on make-up counters herself, and posts 'Get ready with me' make-up tutorials and now dispenses fashion and beauty advice in Grazia Magazine too. Tanya is engaged to Jim and the two of them live together in Norwich. She has her own range of cosmetics, and has published a beauty guide called Love, Tanya.

>:BUSTA MOVE! :<

Silly Dance Moves

Alfie did gymnastics as a kid, and although he can't do the splits any more, he's still pretty good with the dance moves, and has done a few YouTuber Dance Battles against pals like Jim Chapman and Marcus Butler. Here are some Alfie-style dance steps for you to try at home...

1

2

3

4

5

6

7

8

THE CRACKER CHALLENGE

While Alfie has done many different styles of challenges and pranks, some of the best ones have been the ones involving food...

How many dry crackers do you think you could eat in a minute? Try with friends to see who can manage the most (quick tip – have a drink of water beforehand as crackers are very, very dry!) in 60 seconds.

If you're not sick of crackers after the minute challenge, try seeing who can fit the most crackers in their mouth at once (or, for a nicer twist, try this with marshmallows instead).

ZALFIE:
True or False

So you think you know everything there is to know about Alfie Deyes and Zoe Sugg? Well, here are some statements about them and their lives. But which ones are true and which ones are false? Give a thumbs up for true and thumbs down for false. See how many you get right and how much of a Zalfie fan you really are! Answers on page 64.

1. If he had been *a girl*, Alfie's parents would have named him BeTH LiLy Deyes.

2. Zoe's first payment from Google for advertising on her vlog was £10.

3. She has three piercings in each ear.

4. Alfie's Pointless book signing at Waterstones in London's Piccadilly attracted so many fans that the book store had to close their doors to control the crowd.

5. Alfie holds the world record for 'most party poppers popped in 30 seconds'.

6. Alfie's mum calls Alfie and Zoe together 'Zalfie'.

7. Zoe's first popular vlog was '60 Things In My Bedroom'.

8. When Alfie pretended to have a poo facial, he used Marmite instead.

9. Zoe worked as an apprentice at a DESIGN COMPANY before she started her blog.

10. She loves shopping for sunglasses.

11. Zoe's book *Girl Online* was the fastest-selling book of 2014.

12. Her guinea pigs are called PIPPIN AND PERCY.

13. Zoe can speak Greek.

14. Zoe's beauty products include a make-up bag that says 'Just Say No' on the front.

15. Alfie and Zoe performed as part of Band Aid 30 along with Ellie Goulding, Rita Ora and One Direction. Is it true that Adele was also there?

16. Zoe used to SUCK HER THUMB.

17. The first make up Zoe bought was glittery white dazzle dust.

18. Alfie's favourite takeaway is pizza.

19. When Alfie was growing up, he wanted to be a doctor.

20. Zoe's not the only member of her family to have a social media following – as well as her brother Joe's vlog, her GRANDFATHER has an Instagram account called grandadchippy.

BFFs A guide to

A lfie and Zoe are great friends, and they each have really close friends too. Here are some of their secrets to having terrific friendships...

FEELING SHY AND MAKING FRIENDS

If you're starting a new school, or job, it can often be really scary meeting new people and trying to make friends. Just remember pretty much everyone felt the same on their first day too. If you're naturally shy, set yourself a task that you'll start one conversation a day with someone new and it won't be long before you know everyone and have made some great new friends! If you really feel there's no one around that has the same likes and dislikes as you, think about joining a club doing something you enjoy, and you'll find a friend there who loves it too!

DON'T COMPARE YOURSELF TO OTHERS

Some people are naturally outgoing and have loads of friends, other people are more shy and have a few select friendships. It doesn't matter whether you have one friend or 100, it's more important that you're a good friend to those you do have, and that they know they can count on you, and vice versa. So if your best friend has 20 other friends, and you don't, don't be jealous – be pleased that you've got a friend who's popular because they are such a great person to be around!

good friends

STEP AWAY FROM THE COMPUTER/ PHONE/LAPTOP!

While it is great fun chatting to friends online, and texting them, too, if they live round the corner don't forget to put down the electronics sometimes and actually talk face to face! While technology has made it so easy for us to talk to people near and far, sometimes talking to someone in person is the only time you'll really find out how they are feeling – we can all put on a brave face for the camera no matter how bad we feel inside, but it's much harder to fake happiness with a friend in person when what you really need is a good old chummy chat.

MAKE TIME FOR THE PEOPLE WHO MATTER

As you get older you may find the close friends you had when you were younger aren't as close anymore. Sometimes it is because you develop different interests – after all, while we all liked much the same things at the age of five, by the time we are teenagers we like lots of different things. You may still have a lot in common, though, so if you feel a friend is drifting away, the best thing you can do is tell them or arrange a get-together. It could be that they are going through a confusing time, or have been really busy with work, so haven't noticed that you've not spent any time together.

The A–Z Wordsearch

CAN YOU FIND ALL THE WORDS IN THE GRID?

They can be forwards, backwards, up, down or diagonal.

Answers on page 64.

P	g	S	P	O	i	n	t	L	e	S	S
L	R	R	A	t	t	e	k	S	A	Z	B
R	B	A	A	t	B	g	A	i	O	L	S
A	v	m	n	A	A	A	n	e	R	t	t
L	P	u	t	k	j	A	L	L	O	L	H
A	L	e	o	n	e	L	u	n	m	m	u
Z	A	c	n	g	A	F	u	n	A	D	m
j	y	R	o	k	m	m	e	v	k	v	B
F	R	L	H	n	e	S	k	y	e	D	S
e	v	O	L	e	c	k	L	A	u	u	u
e	v	A	L	S	t	o	n	e	P	e	P
e	A	v	L	e	n	i	L	n	o	t	A
O	D	y	A	L	f	i	e	n	y	u	O

ZOELLA Beauty

Zoe's YouTube and blogging journey started with beauty tips and make-up tutorials – first she watched other people's and then she started doing them herself. With her flawless make-up, it's no surprise that Zoe's beauty tips and recommendations have become favourites for her fans, and she even has her own brilliant product range. Here are just some of her best beauty tips:

Don't ASSUME that just because a make-up brand is expensive, it is better than the cheaper ones...

Make-up

The most important thing about make-up is to have fun with it! If you're not sure what colours suit you, or find it difficult to choose a foundation or lipstick shade that's right, take a friend with you when you are make-up shopping for a second opinion. And don't assume that just because a make-up brand is expensive, it is better than the cheaper ones – some of Zoe's favourite products are ones you can buy in your local supermarket or chemist.

Make up essentials
Concealer
Liquid foundation or powder
Bronzer or blusher
Eyeshadow
Mascara
Lipstick or lip gloss

get THE look:

FOR A LOOK THAT WORKS FOR DAYTIME, begin by applying liquid concealer on any blemishes, red areas, or dark under-eye circles.

Blend in the concealer using a medium-sized brush, then, using a larger brush, apply foundation to your face, making sure you have an even finish and carry the colour past your face to your neck. Hopefully it will match your skin colour so it will blend in easily!

If you find cream/liquid foundation too heavy or have oily skin, use a facial powder instead. Then, using a large brush, apply a light dusting of bronzer to your cheekbones, under your cheek and your forehead and blend it in.

Now it's time to apply eye make-up. If you need to, fill in your eyebrows with an eyebrow pencil to match the shade of your brows. Otherwise just run a brush over them or use clear mascara on them to make them neat and tidy.

Go for a natural powder shade on your eyelids, blended in with a small brush, and then apply a darker shade to the crease above your eyelids. You can apply a smokier colour along the lash line with a fine brush.

↓

Then apply mascara. If you want it on your lower lashes, do those first, and then brush your upper lashes. Don't pump the mascara brush into the bottle like they do in the movies – this actually just pushes air into the bottle and dries out your mascara quicker!

↓

Last, but not least, apply a natural pink shade of lip gloss that suits your skin tone. AND YOU'RE READY FOR THE DAY!

FOR MORE GLAMOROUS NIGHT-TIME MAKE-UP, apply concealer and foundation as before.

↓

Choose either a bronzer and apply as you would for the day, or a subtle pink or peach powder blusher to blend in just above your cheekbones. Use a circular motion with your brush when you do this, rather than an up and down motion that will give you pink stripes!

↓

Apply eye make-up as you would during the day but choose stronger colours – if you were using nudes and pale browns for daytime, switch to a beige base colour and more dramatic darker brown for evening, and if you were using pale greys during the day, use a pale grey as your base but then add charcoal in the crease and black eye liner.

↓

Don't forget some dramatic black mascara, too.

↓

Finish up with a darker lipstick or gloss than you would wear during the day.

10 things Every Girl Should Have In Her (VERY BIG) Bag

Deodorant spray or TOP TIP! Get some of those free mini perfume samples from department stores and have one with you in case you need to freshen up during the day

Make-up essentials such as concealer, lip gloss and balm

Dry shampoo – perfect if you have been to the gym or done PE and don't have time to style your hair

Mints or chewing gum for fresh breath

A SMALL BOTTLE OF WATER

Hand sanitiser – handy if you can't wash your hands!

Hairbands or clips just in case you are having a bad hair day!

HAIRBRUSH

Hand cream – especially in cold weather when your skin is drier

Tissues and/ or wet wipes

ZOELLA Beauty

Skincare

Having a good skincare regime can really make a
difference to your make-up. First of all, you need to decide
what skin type you have as that will help you to choose
what products you need. If you're not sure, go to one of the
skincare counters in your local department store or make-
up shop, and chat to the assistants there – and don't feel
you have to buy anything! You can always ask for a sample
of moisturiser or cleanser to see if it is the one for you.

Skincare essentials
Eye make-up remover
Facial wash or cleanser
Facial scrub
Toner
Moisturiser with SPF

If you have dry or sensitive skin

Use a gentle cleanser formulated for dry skin, preferably one without perfumes that can irritate. You may find a creamy cleanser works best, as it won't dry out your skin. Follow with a gentle toner and moisturiser for dry skin.

If you have oily or combination skin

Go for an oil-free face wash or cleanser – ones with the ingredient salicylic acid are good for oily skin. The most important step with oily skin is to cleanse properly. If you are prone to breakouts, choose a face wash for acne or one containing tea tree as this can help pimples from recurring. Don't skip moisturiser because your skin is oily or combination – it's very important to protect your skin and there are many moisturisers especially for your skin type.

Once you know your skin type, it's time to work out what products you need. Zoe often reminds viewers that one of the most important things to do is remove your make-up at night before you go to bed, so a good face wash or cleanser and eye make-up remover is essential. You don't want any mascara smears on your pillow!

In the morning, wash or cleanse your face again and follow it with some toner wiped over your face with a cotton wool pad. Two to three times a week, you can use an exfoliating facial scrub instead of a wash/cleanser to really make sure your skin is as fresh as possible. Do be gentle, though, Zoe advises you shouldn't over scrub.

Then comes moisturiser, preferably with an SPF to protect you from the weather and, if you have sensitive or dry skin near your eyes, you can use an eye cream. Make sure you have clean hands when applying.

41

Whipped Cream
Challenge

Alfie and Zoe once asked each other questions, and if the other person got the question wrong they got covered in a face full of whipped cream.

Take it in turns to ask each other questions to find out how well you really know each other. For example – what's my favourite colour? How old was I when I got my ears pierced? Who is my secret celebrity crush?

If your friend gets the question about you right, they get to eat a treat (maybe a chocolate or piece of fruit). But if they get the question wrong, you get to splat them with whipped cream! For a less messy version of the game, they could eat something a little less tasty – how about a bite of raw chilli, or a chocolate biscuit dipped in Marmite? (Don't pick anything too nasty, like sour milk, though, as you don't want to be sick!)

And then it's your turn...!

Relationships ♥♡

Zoe and Alfie are a happy couple because they support each other, have fun and are thoughtful in their relationship, too. Of course, they've both been in relationships before that haven't worked so well – Zoe has mentioned a bad break-up she had a few years ago – but that means they've had lots of experience of both the good and the bad and have some great advice for all of us!

BE YOURSELF

Zoe's advice is to be yourself. It's simple but it's really true. If someone likes you for you, that's perfect – if you have to change the way you are or the way you behave to get someone to like you, they're not worth your time! Have fun with your friends but don't worry about forcing a relationship – if it is meant to be, it will be!

DON'T FORGET YOUR FRIENDS!

One thing Alfie has mentioned in the past is that it is really important in relationships not to forget your friends just because you have a new boyfriend or girlfriend. Sometimes two people become a couple and stop seeing their friends, which isn't a good idea – especially because it is those exact same friends that you'll need to pass the tissues if your relationship comes to an end! Always make time for your other half, but don't take your friends for granted, either. They'll be there for you forever!

BE THOUGHTFUL

You don't need to shower your boyfriend or girlfriend with expensive gifts to show how much you care about them – little thoughtful gestures mean so much more, whether it's popping by with a takeaway when they are bogged down with work, or offering to take their dog for a walk when they don't feel well. It sounds obvious but it's really true – little things do mean a lot!

DON'T STALK!

If you're in a new relationship, it's understandable that you'll want to know what your boyfriend or girlfriend is doing every single minute of the day when you're not with them. And with today's technology you can find out! But don't. Don't stalk your other half on Twitter, text them every five minutes, or check their Facebook status to see what they're doing and who they are doing it with. It's suffocating for them, and not healthy for you and can lead to a nasty attack of the green-eyed monster. Take a step back and remember, your partner has chosen to be with you, not some clingy, jealous, stalkery person! Try to trust them – trust is one of the most important parts of any relationship.

BAD BREAK-UPS

Not all relationships last, and sometimes you have to accept that yours isn't working. Zoe has talked about bad break-ups and relationships online with Louise in ChummyChatter, and the two of them agree that you have to try to move on, no matter how hard it is. You can't change people, so if it's not working, admit defeat, gather your friends around you and remember that even a bad experience is an experience that will help you learn in life, and it will make you appreciate the great person that will come along in the future.

ALFIE'S POINTLESS GUIDE TO LIFE

Alfie has a very positive outlook on life and has fun when he can. Check out some of his tips to making your day brighter and try them yourself...

1. Don't worry, be happy! Try not to worry about everything - things happen for a reason and shape who we are, and we can't control events

2. Don't play it safe - try new things

3. Go for it. If you want to succeed, you have to try!

4. Build your own dreams, instead of someone else's. Make your own dreams and don't let anyone deter you from achieving your goals!

5. Live in the moment

6. Challenge yourself and don't give up!

7. Don't take life too seriously

8. Make someone smile every day - and try to smile yourself too!

9. Always look on the bright side of life. So you've had a bad haircut - now you have an excuse to rock a really cool hat!

10. If you're not having a good day, promise yourself that you'll do something fun before you go to sleep to cheer yourself up

WOOPIE

vagarious

The DICTIONARY CHALLENGE

W₂ ith a friend, grab a dictionary or go online and find a good dictionary website. Take it in turns to choose a really strange, unusual word and let the other person try to guess what it means. Score one point for each correct answer, and two points for every wrong, but amazingly inventive, answer!

ABSQUATULATE

thrutch

SHALLOP

flocculent

Playing Dress-Up with

ALFIE

Z oe and Alfie both have their own sense of style – and now you can choose what they wear!

Carefully cut out the pieces and then help Alfie get dressed!

alfie essentials

T-shirt

Hat for bad hair days

Jeans

Hooded zip-up sweatshirt

Trainers

49

ZOELLA

Style Essentials: GET THE LOOK!

Want to try out Zoella's fashion style? Well, when you're petite like Zoe – she's 5 ft 4 inches and wears a size 6 to 8 – you have to work out what clothes and hairstyles suit you just as much as someone who is taller or a larger size. If you're petite, loose or baggy clothes just don't work, while if you're tall, crop tops and skater skirts look like you've borrowed your little sister's clothes! Zoe's got it spot on, of course, whether she's dressing for her holidays, a night out or just recording her vlog at home. Read on to find out how you can capture her style for yourself...

Zoella Essentials

Crop tops
Pretty details (flowers, Peter Pan collars)
Bursts of colour
A black or white blazer
Jeans
Little skirts
Hair curlers

DAYTIME

Zoe is a fan of high-street stores like Zara, Primark and Topshop, and loves a bit of online shopping at websites like ASOS.com, too. During the day, she tends to wear jeans or leggings teamed with **pretty blouses** and tops that often have sweet details such as a flower print or lace collar. She loves crop tops, batwing sleeves, high-waisted trousers and often shops in Miss Selfridge as they have cute dresses in petite sizes. 'My style is so varied – I like monochrome and wearing a baggy t-shirt with some Converse or Vans, but I also love girly shirts and dresses,' she told fashion website Lolaandgrace. 'And I own too many Peter Pan collars for my own good!'

HOLIDAYS

A fan of crop tops and **shorts** in hot weather, Zoe also makes sure she takes lots of lightweight t-shirt dresses, pretty skirts and lace tops on her holidays. Of course, her suitcase also has cover-ups and bikinis for the beach, as well as flat sandals – ideal for walking the cobbled streets of the Greek island Santorini, where she went on her holidays!

EVENING

When she goes out in the evening, Zoe often teams a short skirt or **printed shorts** with a fitted top and heels. Most of the time she wears quite understated jewellery, but occasionally she'll brighten up a plain evening outfit with a big statement necklace. She's also a big fan of **blazers** to complete an evening look and has a black one and a white one so there's one to suit any outfit. Zoe has admitted she gets some style inspiration from TV presenter Caroline Flack, who is known for her love of evening shorts that show off her legs.

HAIRSTYLES

ZOE

Blessed with long brown hair (sometimes cut a bit shorter), Zoe is able to try lots of different hairstyles. On holiday, when she lets her hair dry naturally after a dip in the pool or the sea, she often ties back the top of her hair so it's not in her face, and lets the rest of her wavy hair hang free.

To achieve this at home, wash your hair and pat gently with a towel to dry it a little, then add some hair conditioning oil to tame any frizz. If your hair is very tangled, gently brush or comb it, and then run your hands through it to soften it, before leaving your hair to dry naturally. And you're done!

Zoe often has a fringe, but quite a long one so she can flick it to one side. Because her hair is long, she can wear it many different ways – in a bun or ponytail, or loose. She also likes curling her hair to give wavy locks. Even if you have shoulder-length hair, this is a look that will work for you.

Wash and dry your hair as normal. Work some mousse into your hair – preferably one that holds curls – and then, starting at the back of your neck, take small sections of hair and curl each one around a heated curling brush or tong that you're holding vertically.

Hold the hair on the brush/tong for just a few seconds and then let it fall. Repeat this throughout your hair – you'll find it easiest to start at the bottom, at the back of your head, and work your way up, and then do each side in the same way.

Leave the top and front until last so you can decide if you want your hair to have a side parting or not. And be very careful curling your fringe, if you have one – just do little sections for about a second each, as otherwise you'll end up with a big sausage fringe!

Once you have finished curling your hair, leave it to cool for a few minutes before gently running your hands through it to soften the curls. And if you don't have a heated brush or tong, don't worry – grab a circular brush when your hair is wet and dry sections of your hair into curls as described above and hold each one in a Velcro hair roller while you are drying. Once your hair is completely dry and in rollers remove each one gently and you'll have lovely wavy hair.

ALFIE

Alfie's style is easy to achieve if you have short hair. Get a little bit of gel and run your hand through your hair. Then sweep up and across for some volume at the front!

Playing Dress-Up with ZOELLA

Have some fun going through Zoella's fabulous wardrobe and choose her outfit. Carefully cut out the pieces and play dress up!

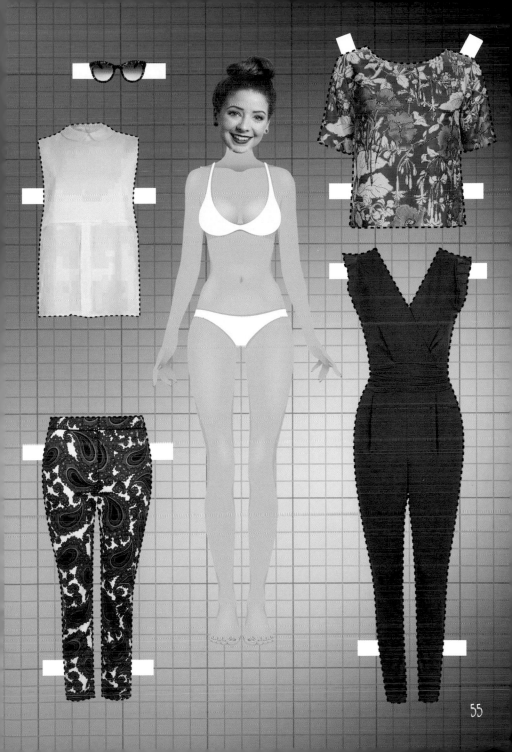

Inside ALFIE's Room

Zoe has had some influence on Alfie's style – you can spot some of her décor in the background of his vlogs! – but while Alfie says that Zoe is messy, his room is always neat and tidy, at least until he starts having fun with his friends!

alfie's room essentials

WOOD FURNITURE AND ACCESSORIES
CANDLES
PLAIN, SIMPLE WALLS AND BEDDING
GADGETS
A LARGE POSTER OR PIECE OF ART

ALFie's Stuff

Like most boys, Alfie is a fan of gadgets and most important is his TV. But there are plenty of other bits and pieces in his room, from his deer antler poster to his BiKe, low lights and candles, and the table that he and his friends have used for lots of pranks... when they're not eating at it, of course.

Most of Alfie's furniture is wood, including a cool stepladder-style shelving unit that holds a few books, CAMERAS and other useful items. He prefers to keeps things plain and simple – maybe so it's easy to clean up when there's been a messy prank!

Get the look

Have a look around your room – does it need a bit of a de-clutter? Putting clothes away and throwing out things you don't want or need (or, even better, donating them to charity) will help you on your way to a clean, crisp-looking room, just like Alfie's.

Once you've tidied things away, all you need is pale, preferably white, walls and some wooden shelving for a few select items that you want on display. A few candles dotted around look nice even if you never light them (and make sure that if you do light a candle you never leave it unattended and you blow it out before you leave the room or go to bed), along with any books you want to have near, and useful things like your PHONE, camera, computer or tablet. All these items look like works of art in themselves, so they make nice ornaments when you're not using them!

Go for plain bed sheets/duvet cover in either grey or white, and then add a dramatic POSTER to inject some interest and colour into the room. It could be from a movie you like, or a print of a piece of art, or maybe you can draw something yourself and put it in a frame? The larger the better, as the rest of your room will be so neat, it will add some real interest to the space.

Inside ZOELLA'S Room

Zoe moved to a flat in the seaside town of Hove, next to Brighton, in February 2014. She injected it with her own sense of style, mixing pale colours with brights, and adding quirky pieces of furniture and accessories. And when Zoe moved in with Alfie eight months later, she brought her style with her!

Spare Bedroom

This is the room we know best, of course, as this is where Zoe records her Zoella vlogs. Like her own bedroom, the walls are pale, and she has a grey accent thanks to a lamp by the bed. The bed itself has some gorgeous purple cushions and pretty fairy lights woven in and around the bed's headboard. The bed always looks neat and nicely made – maybe Zoe is waiting to invite us to be her next house guest?

GET THE LOOK!

Once again, this is an easy look to recreate as most of the colour comes from accessories in the room.

Just choose a bright colour like pink or purple and dot a few accessories – pillows, blanket, candles, even jewellery – around the room.

Walls and bed linen should be kept pale or white, and to add warmth, string some pretty fairy lights around your bed or around the bedroom window.

Bedroom

We don't see it often in her vlogs as she tends to film in her spare room, but Zoe's bedroom is lovely and calm with white walls and a bed with a grey headboard and white sheets. She's brought sunshine into the room with splashes of yellow, from pillows and a blanket on the bed that are yellow and grey, to a yellow drawer in her dresser, and a yellow vase on top of it. Our favourite accessory, though, has to be the panda pillowcase on her bed – and he even has a yellow bow tie! Zoe loves her colour scheme so much it is also used in her living room where she had a giant grey sofa, yellow floor lamp and a custard cream cushion.

Zoella's room essentials

Accessories in bright colours.
Pretty lights and lamps
Cushions and pillows
Neutral coloured walls and furniture
Fun neutral coloured patterns and designs

GET THE LOOK!

You can make your bedroom as fresh and fun as Zoe's in a few simple steps.

First, see if it is okay to paint your bedroom walls white, and perhaps get a few adults to help as it can get messy! Then choose a subtle colour such as grey, beige, or a pale mint and find some accessories in this colour. It could be a leftover piece of fabric you can use to make cushion covers or a headboard cover, a lampshade no one is using or a blanket.

Then pick a bright colour that will go with your subtle shade. For example, Zoe has put yellow with grey but orange would also have worked, and orange or red works with beige, while a deep blue would look lovely with mint green. Again, any accessories or bits of leftover fabric you can use to decorate would be great – maybe you have a bright t-shirt you no longer wear that you could cut up and use to cover a small cushion?

And if you have a chest of drawers or a vase you can paint, just buy one of those sample paint pots in the colour you like and paint a drawer, or ornament, to add colour to the room.

THE ultimate ZALFIE QUIZ

T hink you know everything about Zoella and Alfie? Then take the quiz below to find out how much you really know about our favourite vlogging couple... **Answers on page 64.**

1) Why does Zoe like having size 3 feet?

a) they're small enough that Alfie can't accidentally step on them
b) she can buy shoes in the children's section
c) there are always size 3 shoes left in the sales
d) she can borrow her best friend Louise's shoes as they are the same size

2) Which boardgame does Alfie think he rules at?

a) Scrabble
b) Cluedo
c) Monopoly
d) Snakes and Ladders

3) Zoe used to pretend she couldn't swim at school because:

a) she didn't want to have to go underwater and get her hair wet
b) she can't swim!
c) she didn't like wearing a swimsuit
d) she was worried someone had peed in the pool!

4) Which of these things does Alfie say he can't do?

a) he can't dance
b) he can't wink
c) he can't whistle
d) he can't tie his shoelaces

5) Which TV series did Zoe appear in as an extra?

a) *Eastenders*
b) *Downton Abbey*
c) *Cranford*
d) *Hollyoaks*

6) What happened to Alfie's childhood snake Smidge?

a) Alfie gave him back to the pet shop because he was tough to look after
b) He died
c) He disappeared one day and Alfie thinks he went down the toilet
d) He went to live at London Zoo

7) Which TV presenter does Zoe have a crush on?

a) Noel Edmonds
b) Graham Norton
c) Jonathan Ross
d) Phillip Schofield

8) There is a video of Alfie when he was little doing something embarrassing. What is it?

a) he's wearing a dress and dancing to the Spice Girls
b) he's on a potty
c) he's dressed up as Peppa Pig and singing the theme song
d) he's got long hair and his mum is plaiting it into pigtails

9) What make-up skill is Zoe rubbish at?

a) applying false eyelashes
b) applying false nails
c) giving herself a pedicure
d) applying eyeliner

10) What happened when Alfie shaved his head for charity when he was 13?

a) he wore a hat for weeks afterwards
b) he cried
c) he bought a bright red wig and wore it to school
d) he kept it shaved for a year because he liked it so much

11) How many times did Zoe have to take her driving test before she passed?

a) she passed first time
b) she passed on the second try
c) she took her test three times
d) she hasn't passed her driving test yet

12) Which of these naughty things did Alfie do when he was little?

a) he shaved a circle into his dad's hair when his dad was asleep
b) he stole a sweet from the local sweet shop and blamed his sister
c) he hid his pet snake in his mum's underwear drawer to scare her
d) he took a neighbour's dog for a walk and lost it in the park

13) What was Zoe's favourite subject at school?

a) PE
b) art
c) languages
d) maths

14) Which of these musicals did Alfie *not* appear in at school?

a) *Fiddler on the Roof*
b) *Jesus Christ Superstar*
c) *West Side Story*
d) *Annie*

15) What TV series does Zoe love so much she thinks she has seen every episode at least 10 times?

a) *The Big Bang Theory*
b) *The Inbetweeners*
c) *Friends*
d) *Sex and The City*

The Future

So what's next for vlogging superstars Alfie and Zoe? As their Pointlessblog and Zoella subscriber numbers rise daily, the sky is really the limit for the two online, and there's lots to come for both of them away from YouTube too. Zoe is working with MIND charity as a digital ambassador talking about anxiety and panic attacks, they've moved to new house and their second books will both be coming out.

They've travelled the world, sung with some of the world's most famous popstars, and launched books and beauty ranges, but still managed to stay down to earth. Still only in their early twenties, there is plenty of time for both Zoe and Alfie to follow their dreams and think of new ones – maybe Zoe will return to acting or Alfie will launch a clothing line (or maybe hair products!) ... whatever they decide to do, alone and together, we're sure it will be fun, cool and amazing!

Answer Page

Page 19 – The 1-Minute Spot the Difference Challenge

Page 30 – The A-Z Wordsearch

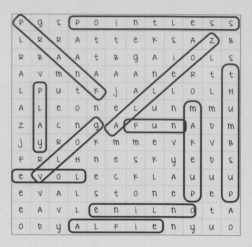

Page 26 – Zalfie: True or False?

1. True. 2. False, it was £60. 3. False,
she only has one piercing in each ear. 4.
True, 8000 fans showed up. 5. False, Alfie
did hold the record, but it was broken
by Ashrita Furman in October 2013. 6.
True. 7. True. 8. False, it was Nutella. 9.
True. 10. False, Zoe says because she has
a small head she finds it impossible to
get sunglasses that fit. 11. True. 12. True.
13. False, but she does have an A-level in
French! 14. False, it says 'Just Say YES'.
15. False, Adele didn't attend. 16. True.
17. True. 18. False – he loves Chinese. 19.
False, he wanted to be a dentist. 20. True.

Page 60 – The Ultimate Zalfie Quiz

1.	b	9.	a
2.	c	10.	b
3.	a	11.	c
4.	b	12.	a
5.	c	13.	b
6.	a	14.	d
7.	d	15.	c
8.	a		

With thanks to Evie Hayes, a very special fan.